When you've exhausted your all,
that's when you ...

DIE
EMPTY
WHILE
LIVING A
FULL LIFE

DIE EMPTY WHILE LIVING A FULL LIFE
Copyright © 2021 by Julius Hammond

All scriptures are from the Kings James Version (KJV) of the Bible, except otherwise stated.

DIE EMPTY WHILE LIVING A FULL LIFE

ISBN: 978-1-932448-23-8 (Paperback)
Available in Kindle, eBook

Published By:
BuddleWriter
www.giannahsmith.com

JULIUS HAMMOND

When you've exhausted your all,
that's when you ...

DIE
EMPTY
WHILE
LIVING A
FULL LIFE

Dedication

This book is dedicated to my Almighty, Savior, Elohim, Yeshua; the divine master and creator of my identity and destiny.

Table of Contents

---⊙---

Introduction

L ife is often referred to as a game, and if life is a game, our experiences are like the cards the dealer deals. In my 37 years on earth, I have learned to embrace every card and give my all in every round. So far, I have grown to equally appreciate every result, whether it is a loss or a win. For there is no such thing as failure; I either learn or win!

Many of the experiences I have been afforded were not what I expected, and frankly, they were not ones I would have chosen for myself. My life so far feels like I have gone to the moon and back, feeling emotions I have never felt before, touching the lives of people I have never met, seeing things I never dreamt of, and overcoming in ways I never thought possible.

The layers of my journey are mixed with trials and learning, always toward a win. Like the wind, the trials came fast and furious, without time or a moment to identify where they were coming from and where they would take me. Yet even when my stand was weak, I knew one day I would triumph and stand to tell my story. That day has finally arrived!

As I reflect, back then, it seemed every experience resembled the other, as if I was being dealt the same set of cards over and over again. I was crushed many times, and sometimes I swore I would never play another round. But life does not make deals with us. Its purpose is to teach us and provide those nuggets of wisdom along the way. So, very early, I realized that to learn, I would need to give every round of play my best shot at winning, even if it took me faking it until I made it.

Giving my all was not always easy; after every round, I felt like a failure, and my caution would kick in. I wanted so badly to *"take sleep and mark death,"* but life provided cushions of comfort and glimpses of hope to help me get ahead. Life taught me to give my all, even when I was all I had to give. That is why I now show up full and leave empty, for it means I've added value rather than numbers. Myles Munro said, *"The graveyard is the richest place on the surface of the earth because there you will see the books that were not published, ideas that were not harnessed, songs that were not sung, and drama pieces that were never acted."*

II

Holding back in fear will
always keep us from
shinning in the light of
our destiny.

- JULIUS HAMMOND

So, as you read every chapter of my story, embrace the knowledge that every experience is meant to increase you in wisdom and stature. For our experiences guarantee us a sense of wisdom that we can only be acquired from a place of gratitude and godly understanding. Know that when you give your best uncompromisingly, you will gain a rare wisdom that only experience could have taught you. For only then, will you be able to truly choose to die empty rather than full.

Preface

As far back as I can recall, I remember being part of a loving, close knitted family. However, in my reflection, a significant part of my childhood and young adult memory represented a life lived in two extremes. And a thin line separated both. Everything was defined, hot or cold, love or hate; there was no room or time for indecision, lukewarm efforts, or emotional confrontation. Life was going to be life, and I had to learn not just to live it but own it.

I was told that my birth was the start of an evolution for my extended family. I was the first child for my parents and the first grandchild for both sets of my grandparents. My mother's family was like the 'Soul Food' family of the nineties. The dinners at grandmas were frequent, and everyone was excited to come to the weekend barbecues, no matter how often. My mother talked to her parents every day, and they made it their duty to share what was happening in each other's lives. For them, family was about being there for each other, whether we were needed or not. When I tell people, I was not just loved; I knew I was loved, they always ask for an explanation. Then, I would explain: To be loved is very different from knowing that you are loved. The difference resided in the way it was communicated. My mother's parents adored me, and they showed it every day.

Like roads with potholes, so are families with anomalies. I knew my mother's parents loved me. I also knew my father's mother greatly disliked me because she disliked my mother. That was the result of an issue my father failed to address, even to his death. He tended to favor my grandmother more. That fostered many relationship problems between my mother and my father's mother. Yes, both families uncompromisingly showed their love or great dislike, no middle ground. If they loved you, you knew, and if they did not, you knew that too.

Besides the obvious unwavering loyalty to one thing or another, I was blessed with the balance of both sides of the fence. One set of grandparents seemed to balance out the other, which now, I believe to be a blessing. For, as one showered me with love and supported my development, the other challenged my confidence and perception of self-worth.

As time would tell, death came and stayed a long while with us, unlike most families. For some families, it is years of battling illnesses, one behind the other, but for my family, we buried the dead, one behind the other. The experience mortified and changed me. Each death revealed the depth of life's realities and the raw value of having each person added. Those experiences came with much learning. Though perhaps disappointing to say, it took death for me to realize that giving of myself must be uncompromised and complete in every way. I have learned that if I gave my best efforts in all my endeavors, I would have given something much greater to others.

The application of learning produces wisdom.

- JULIUS HAMMOND

So far in life, I have been a son, brother, grandson, father, husband, business partner, and author. Still, I believe there is more inside of me to give because Julius Hammond is not yet empty!

CHAPTER 1

Who AM I?

In hindsight, I thank God I got the privilege to grow up and live with my parents and grandparents because those memories have given me firsthand knowledge of where I came from. During those years, the reality of what life entailed was berry shaped in each interaction day-by-day. It was not until I became an adult that I understood the difference between who I was and who I have become.

'Who I was' represents the veil of my identity. It is the question that should reveal the definition of conditioning and ideologies. It represents my inherited identity, an image of resemblance to family, genes, and generational blessings and curses. It represents the part of me the world saw at birth until I began to evolve into the real me. 'The me' with a defined purpose and promise.

To arrive at my destination, I understood that I needed to know where I came from; thus, my first step was to identify who I was. The journey of answering the of *'who I am?'* involved reflecting on where I came from geographically and demographically and embracing the gifts and character traits given to me through my DNA.

As human beings, we are identified by our parents' names at birth. Yet, often it seems we have no identity other than the one we are given through our family. Nevertheless, we are born with a unique identity that manifests itself through the trials and tribulations of life.

On March 30th, 1984, in Gardena, California, I was born to Wendy Nunn and Joe Lee Hammond Jr. I was named Julius Hammond, but very soon, unique quirks and tendencies began to peek through, earning me various nicknames along the way.

My birth brought my parents immense joy. They tried to continue the legacy of a close-knitted family, but their efforts were met with many challenges. The challenges stemmed from my father's side of the family. That was primarily because my father's mother greatly disliked his wife (my mother). That put a strain on my parents' marriage and contributed to their divorce. By that time, I was eight (8) years old.

On the surface, it seemed like nothing significant had caused the breakup of our family. However, a closer look showed me that my father did not leave (his mother and father) and cleave to his wife. My father allowed many of his decisions pre and post-marriage to be dictated by my grandmother. My grandmother's dislike was the seed planted, and my father's actions continued to water the lurking separation in his marriage. In many ways, my mother's needs and desires were treated as minor, while my grandmother's needs were prioritized. In hindsight, watching them interact, I can see that the fragmentation of our family began in the foundation. Based on this knowledge, I have consciously decided to maintain good relations with my in-laws and take the responsibility to leave and cleave to my wife more seriously.

While growing up, I loved to play sports. I was involved in almost all school sports-related activities: basketball, baseball, football, etc. My father was at every game, cheering me along in the crowd. I didn't know what loss was really like because my father made every occasion a win and an opportunity to teach me a life lesson about focus and endurance. That is something I admired about my father, and it is something I have chosen to keep as part of my identity as a father.

At birth, I was born with my God-given identity, though it took years to be identified and is still being unveiled. Being born into this family meant I took on its history and legacy. Yet, through the influence of my parents, I also learned to look at and live life differently. As a teen, even when I wanted to be negative, I couldn't because my father was so positive. My mother and grandma were so loving; they saw the best in every situation. Again, having them as parents helped form the fabric of my personality, perceptions, and perspectives toward life, which has helped shape my identity today.

I have always believed that my life was a tapestry with parts that complement each other. So, I learned to cope with my grandmother while finding life lessons in the experience. After a while, I learned how to be kind to my grandmother without allowing the hurt she caused to affect me. I learned to embrace my father and mother without taking sides or being angry at my father. What I didn't know at that time was that my actions were separating me from identifying myself with that identity. Although my grandmother and I saw life from different vantage points, it did not stop me from doing good to her. I was no longer judgmental about it. I no longer regarded it. I was no longer hurt about it. In fact, very early, I learned that *"you can lead a horse to the water, but you cannot make it drink."* I understood that my father had decided what was

4

important to him, and we all reaped the consequences daily. Again, through reflection, I recognized that if I wanted better results, I had to do better than my father did. In doing that, I separated myself from that aspect of my family, so I would align with the identity I wanted for my own marriage and family.

I have shared my past with my wife, so she would understand why I do certain things and why I don't do certain things. We committed to making an effort not to relive the past. Instead, we decided to create our own legacy. Through prayer and our consistent efforts, I now share a good relationship with my in-laws.

My mother's mother (my granny) is my fondest memory. She was a ray of hope and possessed a light of love that shone very bright. Perhaps she too decided to unveil the identity God gave her to leave a legacy of togetherness and love to pass on to my sisters and me. My granny fed life and energy into me. She was my' ride or die. She was always there for me, no matter what was happening. When the pressures with my father's mother became overwhelming, her love illuminated my life as light does to a cave. My granny had her own woes, struggles, and otherwise, but she went through with gratitude and courage. I can imagine that as a child and young adult, I did not know everything that happened, but she never allowed her challenges to diminish our relationship. Her legacy has inspired me to make gratitude, faith, and courage a part of my identity. Knowing that I was born with an identity defined by the love of God and anything less than the same would just not be me.

By the time I made the transition into adulthood, I had already developed a positive mindset because of my father's lessons. But nothing could have prepared me for the trials of life that came like a whirlwind, fast and furious, non-stop, over six (6) consecutive years. The losses hit us hard, turning my world upside down. But between the layers of loss was my *'paradigm shift.'* The experience taught me that there is always a benefit in adversity. The trials my family and I went through were indeed very real, but they were trials with silver linings. They were wisdom teaching experiences. They were blessings, shaping my identity.

If you want to define my identity, look at what I give. I can only give what I have. I did not choose my family but growing up with them helped to shape the me God intended. God gave me my identity. And he also gave me a choice to unveil it. That means I had to choose what I received and stored and what I let go of and disregarded. Life involves a series of choices, all holding a certain weight of consequence – live or die, give or receive, faith or fear. Irrespective of what life has to give, our choices determine how we live life.

Have you ever noticed that in the scriptures of the Old Testament, there are numerous accounts of God encouraging several people to *"Fear not."* Yet, in the scriptures of the New Testament, Jesus never once told us to be afraid of any man or situation outside of God in reverence. Instead, he told us to BELIEVE. In Philippians 4:8, the bible urges us to think and gravitate to positivity because our thoughts define what is manifested in our lives. *"For as he thinketh in his heart, so is he..."* Proverbs 23:7. That is because the things we focus on have the creative energy to manifest in our lives. That example in the scriptures has caused me to realize that in establishing a new identity, we must deliberately do the opposite of what we have refused to accept or decide to let go of. Often parents constantly focus on the negative by constantly reminding children what they should not do, instead of highlighting the positive, by telling them what to do. When we let go of the things we do not want and stop regarding them, we will not have the negative to give. Letting go creates a void that must be filled with the things by which we have chosen to be identified. Whatever we choose to identify with is also what we will have to give as a legacy.

Indeed, it is much harder to fit a square peg into a round hole. I was born 'who I am,' yet, my family sometimes tried to shape me into a circle, expecting me to fit into a square. Other times, I was shaped as a square (depending on what/who was at play at the time). In scripture, there are records of persons whose names significantly shaped who they would become. In some instances, the negative experiences persons had been a direct result of their name, and only God's intervention made the difference. Our 'true identity' is not always aligned with the name we are given, but, instead, what we choose to accept for ourselves. It is in the inheritances we choose to receive and make our own and the new legacies we choose to create. I chose to use the knowledge (about where I came from) to determine what I did not want in my life even before the trials came. The knowledge helped me to intentionally remove the veil of resemblance to reveal who I am.

You, too, may have already identified who you are. But for those who have not yet started the journey to the true realization of self, to answer the question 'who am I,' it will take time. Identifying who you are is like peeling back the layers of an onion. It constitutes a slow process that may cause tears, but reaching the core, will be rewarding. The process is one of patience and dedication. Remember, Jesus knew who he was in the spirit (at 12 years old), but he didn't know who he was in the natural until he subjected himself to the period of learning. (If he knew who he was in the natural, he would have acknowledged his earthly father and not his heavenly father when his parents found him teaching at the synagogue). It is only when you finally identify who you are that you live life from an authentic viewpoint.

To see the true reflection of oneself, one must stand in front of the mirror of truth.

- JULIUS HAMMOND

CHAPTER 2

———————————— ☉ ————————————

Layers of Loss

"For whosoever will save his life shall lose it: and whosoever will lose his life for my sake shall find it." –
Matthew 16:25

E very loss brings great gain and much joy in the end. For it is in our willingness to let go of all that we truly find abundance and live a full life. Ask Job (in the scriptures); he will tell you how loss can lead to joy and great gain.

Breakup and Divorce

My parents got married in 1979 and had my sister and me between 1984 and 1986. Our family was characterized by love and a strong bond, but fate played hardball on us. As children, we could see that our parents were friends, but they lacked the intimacy that characterized a strong marriage. Although they were married on paper, my dad did not make it to the place in the traditional vows that said, *"For this reason, shall a man leave his father and mother and cleave to his wife."* As far back as I can remember, my grandmother (father's mother), Delores Hammond, never accepted my mother as his wife. She had a strong dislike for my mother and thought her son could have done better. By age 13/14, I noticed that the energy around my grandmother was always tense. Although she did not say it, but her attitude sent a clear message that my mother was not good enough for my father. Her blank stares shook me, and although my mother was an extremely strong woman, the blatant disrespect hurt her deeply. Sometimes, when she sat with us at home, she seemed so lost, almost like a stranger in a strange place, amongst strangers.

My grandmother's behavior was only one of the causes that added to the break-up of my family. That, among several other things, put a strain on my parents' marriage dynamics from the beginning. My sisters felt it too, but to a lesser extent because they were always focused on school and spent much of their time away from my grandmother.

I spent a lot of time with my father, and his parents were always an added accessory to our daily lives. During those prolonged visits to my father's parents, I recognized my grandmother's deep-seated dislike for me. She disliked me because of my mother but loved my sister from the same mother and father. That also caused me to realize something I did not understand at the time - my grandmother had put more value on a person's accomplishment rather than the person. She viewed things very differently from the way I did. She believed that life was about a person's accomplishments and saw degrees as success and titles as character-defining. As a result, there was a noticeable difference in how she treated my sister versus me. My sister was doing exceptionally well academically. She graduated from university with a degree, and I did not. Thus, my grandmother respected her more than she did me. Although I did not understand my grandmother's way of thinking, I knew it was wrong. Today, I am grateful that irrespective of my accomplishments, the memory is a welcomed reminder that life is about people and that the things we have acquired simply complement the moments we share.

In the early years, my grandmother was the same toward me whether I was doing something for her or not. The name-calling and disrespect were a constant challenge to my self-esteem. As a child, I desired a grandma's love, but she would not be a hypocrite (and be nice), not even when she wanted something from me.

My relationship with my grandmother was very different from my relationship with my grandfather (her husband). They were extremely close and shared a bond in their marriage that seemed exemplary. But they were very different toward me. My grandfather was a loving, kind, and compassionate individual, and as I got older, I got closer to him. Although we had many strong disagreements and discussions, our love for each other was unconditional. However, my grandfather did not involve himself too much in the rift that existed between my mother and grandmother. He always took my grandmother's side. Perhaps, because she was his wife, and he didn't want to make her upset. Sometimes he said certain things in my favor, but he never outrightly defended me. As a child, I did not think he could have changed my grandmother. Now, I understand that they did not know their roles as husband and wife.

My grandfather's silence affected my family and affected his relationship with his son (my father). It was apparent that there were differences between both of them. I did not fully understand the issues as a child. But, later, I understood they were a direct result of my grandfather's response (or passivity) to the issue. It seemed to have deeply hurt my father. Nonetheless, he, too, never defended my mother, not even once. Instead, he, too simply did not respond. I am grateful I was able to witness this. If I didn't, I would not have understood the necessary changes to make in my own family.

Of course, there were other issues in my parents' marriage, but my grandmother was like the straw. A huge straw that was ever-present from the beginning, throughout, until the end – and it broke their marriage. My father never did what my grandmother wanted him to do, and he did not defend his wife and family. Instead, whenever his mother said hurtful things, he comforted me with the word of God. For a while, I wondered why he didn't stop his mother. I stopped wondering as soon as I recognized the good in the experience. Every time my father noticed how hurt I was, he shared a scripture to lift my spirit. That is something I have adopted and paired with practical actions to support my children). The seed of good that he sowed in me helped me be a better person to my grandmother than she was to me. My mother once said to my father, *"your mother is always in our business; she might as well be your wife."* I believe those words cut my father deeper than my mother knew, but I believe that was her intention. He simply did not seem to see how he allowed his mother to hurt the family he was supposed to protect.

The divorce hurt my family greatly, far more than we imagined, and I internalized it all. My parents, sister, and I lived together for only four years. By 1993 my family was no longer together. In the beginning, my sister and I were bouncing between both our parents. Although we deeply loved each other as family, the physical separation made our mother sad for years. She knew she had to let go of the marriage and start a new life, which she did.

Some time passed, then my mother remarried. She was her old self again, blossoming in beauty every day. My father dated a few women, some for several years, but he never committed to marriage again. My mother knew about his relationships, even before she got married, but that did not seem to bother her; I think she felt free. The loss of my parent's marriage created or continued a legacy of martial loss for my sisters and me. We missed the close-knit family that our friends and neighbors enjoyed. I now see the importance of family, and I believe I am blessed to have had the opportunity to change that legacy for my children. My marriage has had setbacks, but my wife and I are stronger now than before. We are committed to watering our marriage with God's unconditional love and his Word.

Our decision to refuse to accept marital loss as a legacy has created a new legacy of marital bliss and oneness for our children and their children.

After a while, my father and I lived together, and my sisters lived with our mother. (At the time I was a teenager, I lived with my mother and her husband, but due to issues in their marriage, I started living with my father full-time). Dad and I had our disagreements, but we also had something he and his father did not have; we were both free to express our feelings and opinions without compromising our love for each other. As a result of my grandmother's behavior, we were careful to protect each other's self-esteem (in whatever way necessary).

***

My father and I continued to live together for a few years. There is a famous saying (often used to promote satisfaction and compromise) – *"better something than nothing."* That saying proved inadmissible in the issue with my grandmother. As she aged and her strength diminished, her attitude improved from zero to twenty percent. <u>Her something was twenty percent, and it was not better than nothing</u>. It only meant she treated me with less disdain. I believe she did this because she realized I was always there, and I saved her money. She became conveniently nice when she wanted me to do something for her. I took her to doctor visits and shopping. I did her laundry and drove her wherever she wanted to go. I do not regret what I did for her, but I did not like how it made me feel at that time. Now, I understand that the experience will always profit me. Although I did not have to do what I did, I am grateful that I did. It represents bread cast on waters (which I will continue to find in my days ahead).

By 1998 My grandparents' health deteriorated rapidly, causing them to become more dependent on my father and me. Things and times were changing, and my grandmother's attitude toward me had changed a little. Our relationship was not mended, but there were small improvements. I think my grandmother realized at that time that my father and I were all they had.

My grandfather had severe Dementia, so he needed help with everything. At night he would forget to go to the bathroom, so he had frequent accidents. He sometimes forgot who I was, even my father's name and where he lived. He could not organize his own medication, so that was something my father and I had to monitor. For relief, my father hired nurses who would assist with his care.

It was not easy to care for two elderly people and maintain a regular life, and so dad and I sacrificed many things to take care of them ourselves. I loved my grandfather and grandmother, but there were days when it became overwhelming. My grandmother was still unkind. I sometimes stayed with friends just to protect my mental stability. But, as they got older and weaker, I knew I could not stay away, regardless.

New Relationship

I n 2004, I met a young woman named Shay Mcguire. We started dating, and our relationship got serious very quickly. By November 2006, we were welcoming our daughter, Samarah, into the world. By 2007 my daughter's mother and I separated due to several unresolved issues. Although my daughter's birth was the catalyst to me becoming a better man, the relationship with her mother was in shambles. I had started a journey of establishing my own family, and in what seemed to be an instant, my family was torn apart. At that time, I thought the breakup happened overnight, but in retrospect, I realized that it happened long before we physically separated.

Although I am married now, the road before true love was a very difficult one. After the separation, I moved to Las Vegas. I needed to get away from it all. I had become a single parent, taking on the role of a full-time father, friend, security, etc., for my daughter. Some nights I watched her sleep and wondered if her life was a repeat of what had happened to me. When my parents separated, having my father in my life made a difference, and I was determined to be there for my little girl.

Mom's Diagnosis

By 2010 my mother was diagnosed with lupus. It changed all of our lives. I lived in Torrance, California, while my mother and sister lived in Las Vegas. Regardless of the distance, we remained very close. My sister was there for her every step of the way.

My grandparents (my mother's parents) taught me the value of dedication to family, a good work ethic, and a wise business mind. So, although I lived in California and they lived in Las Vegas, I was able to provide the financial assistance they needed. I worked as a security guard for eight years for a reasonably good salary ($13 per hour, six days per week).

While I was grateful for my job, I dreamt of becoming an entrepreneur (just like my granddaddy). Thus, I enrolled in a three-year entrepreneur program at Devry University. However, I chose to discontinue my enrollment to take care of my responsibilities as a son and father. My dream to be an entrepreneur did not die, but I knew I needed to focus on supporting my family at that time. I felt it was my time to be a parent to my parents. The example my father had set in being there for his parents prepared me to do the same for them when the time came. I did not for a moment think of myself, school, or my dream career. I knew what a degree could afford me, but my family needed me more at that time. The value of family was embedded in the uncompromising, unconditional love freely given. It is an unwritten principle that comes in the character of those who give the whole, leaving nothing in reserve. It exists with those who understand the difference between deep care and unconditional love. At that time, I was 23 years old, and the legacy of love I received during childhood evidently had continued in my life. Today, the family I have and the success we have achieved is a constant reminder that only in giving will we abundantly receive.

My grandmother's death (Dad's mother)

March 2011, my grandmother died. We had not lost anyone in our family before, and although we knew she was unwell and climbing in age, her death came as a shocker for us. I cannot remember what happened the day before she died, but I will not forget the morning she woke up and could hardly breathe, talk or move. It was a beautiful Saturday morning. We were all home relaxing when my father went in to check on my grandmother. Suddenly our lives changed. My grandmother was unresponsive, and my father was in shock. I immediately went into survival mode, and we hurriedly took her to the hospital. Her kidneys had failed, so the doctors immediately placed her on life support. After one week, the doctors said there was nothing else they could do for her. My grandmother transitioned at 83 years old, out of this life and into the next. Her death was obviously not sudden, but it was still quick. Almost like she was here today and gone tomorrow.

Her death was a surreal experience. I had mixed feelings, ones I could not have explained at that time. Feelings of sadness, and relief, flooded my emotions all at the same time. It was so confusing. I was sad at her passing but free from the rejection and hate. It bothered me for a while, but after a few years and a lot of self-learning, I understood and accepted that my feelings were normal.

By that time, my parents had been divorced for 13 years. As expected, my mother sent her condolences and made herself available to help in any way she was needed. She was a family person, and she loved her family unconditionally (just like her mother). My mother was brought up to put family first, no matter what. So, although she moved on with her personal life, she did not forget that we were all one family. I think that is why she accepted that she could not change her mother-in-law, so she made peace with that situation rather than fighting forever. Regrettably, my mother and grandmother never reconciled their differences. Although I know, I am my mother's child. I also know I have to be my own person, and create my own legacy. Thus, I try to live in peace, love, and harmony with everyone.

2012, One year later...the loss of another

After my grandmother died in 2011, my grandfather deteriorated even further. We knew he needed us more than ever, and we never left his side. The sadness I felt when I realized he, too, would soon transition sent me into denial. I knew I should have prepared for his going, but I could not bring myself to do it.

Although the Dementia he suffered from seemed to worsen, he never once mistook the loss of his wife as anything else. He missed his wife and often said, *"I am ready to go home."* As his health worsened, I still found it hard to accept the reality that he, too, would soon be gone. We had an exceptional bond, which made it harder.

He died on Feb 11, 2012, approximately one year after his wife. Everyone said he died of a broken heart. When he died, I felt the loss was suffocating me. But experiencing his death taught me that I needed to let go. Not just let go of family, but of anything that had expired in my life. For in letting go, I would make room for much greater.

My relationship with my grandmother was a love-hate relationship, so at that time, I thought my grandfather's death was a more significant loss than hers. However, as I got older, I realized that both their lives and death taught me several invaluable lessons, ones I will tell you about later.

Up to this point, I have not shared much about my granny and granddaddy (my mother's parents). My granddaddy had a big heart, and it was the first thing everyone would see when they met him. His wife's heart was twice as big, and she never speared to share it. She was my rock, he was my anchor, and I was their heartbeat. They loved my sister and I unconditionally and provided a love haven for us even when things got tense elsewhere.

My granny and grandad lived in Gardena, California, for a while. Then they moved to Las Vegas, Nevada but eventually settled in Palos Verdes, California, in their later years. Weekends and holidays with them were spectacular. They spoiled me most of my childhood and teenage years, but they never allowed me to get out of line. They taught me to respect myself, be grateful and be happy, no matter what was happening (there was always something happening in our family). I remember my granny and granddad had set up an area in their garage for me to play my video games; my own mini man cave. They did that so I would feel loved and welcomed whenever I visited.

I spent a lot of my toddler to preteen years with them and learned almost all my early business lessons from them. They love me so much, they named their business after me, called Julius House Foundation Incorporated. They started it with my parents in 1988, when I was four years old. It was a group home, and they never passed up an opportunity to take me there. They were delighted to teach my sister and I all the lessons they learned about business and life. They taught us how to do administrative tasks, balance a checkbook, etc. My sister is an expert at accounting and booking keeping today because of lessons from our loving grandma.

During the financial meltdown of 2003, the business suffered financially, and they were forced to close its doors. They not only closed the business, but they also moved to Las Vegas, Nevada. They had a lifestyle change, but it did not change who they were.

My granny loved music; it kept her spirit and her hopes high. She often played her beloved 'I Remember Mama' by Shirley Ceasar. Whether she hummed or sang out loud, her joy would pull everyone around her to sing along as well. She was a lover of what we would now call the old school classics, like music from The O-JAYS, Shirley Ceasar, The Clarke Sisters, and many others from that era. To this day, I still listen to Shirley Ceasar's 'I Remember Mama,' and I still get emotional when I remember how we listened and sang together.

After my dad's parents died, my mother was experiencing some issues with her living situation and needed a place to stay. My father did not hesitate to offer my mother his house to stay. After all, several years had passed since their divorce, and they had settled their differences and became good friends.

Early Sept 2013... Sudden Changes

Dad and Alicia were in the living room watching the television while Mom and Brittany were on their way back from the store. (Brittan is my half-sister by my mother, she was born after my parents divorced.) I distinctly remember my mom calling to say that granddaddy had called to say that granny was not looking good. Before processing the news, mom called back before pulling up at the gate and said granny had fallen and was not breathing.

This felt like lightning was about to strike in the same place. We had just gotten over the loss of my father's parents, and... here came trouble again...If you were there, you would have seen what looked like my mother's heart dropping out of her chest and her quick bounce into leader mode. Being the leader, my mother took the phone and began telling my grandaddy how to resuscitate granny. Remember, my granny was the matriarch/Big Mama of our own 'Soul Food' family. My sisters started panicking, and my mother was on the verge of a breakdown, but just like me, she always goes into solution mode no matter how severe the circumstance. After all, we had endured so much loss, we knew better than to run around frantic in a panic. My mother started to question my granddaddy, who was also out of it. Grandaddy was a brave military veteran who allowed nothing to stand in his way, but that day, he was worried, sick, and shocked, not knowing what to do to help his unresponsive wife (of 55 years), and instead of calling 911, he called my mother.

That day, my grandmother suffered a heart attack, passed out, and fell onto the bathroom floor. In a split second, she died before we even left the house. The news came while mom was on the phone with grandaddy; he was devastated!

It was a devastating blow to my family. I can still remember my parents, my sisters, and I crying in the house that afternoon. At that moment, I felt I was going down the spiral of conscious denial. I knew what was happening, I was mourning, but I wanted to awaken so badly from what seemed to be a bad dream instead of facing such a terribly painful reality. We knew granddaddy needed us, so we pulled ourselves together.

Granny and grandaddy had moved back from Las Vegas to Palos Verdes, but due to unforeseen circumstances, they were now living in a senior community in Long Beach,

California. So, we immediately left Los Angeles for Long Beach, California, to console granddaddy and see granny one last time. It was the longest 40-minutes drive of our lives.

By the time we got there (my aunt and uncle, who as a pastor, coroner, and ambulance were already there), the place was yellow-taped like a crime scene as they processed the body. I was pissed, uneasy, and almost uncooperative. My memories of her flashed before me, and I could not begin to process my life continuing without my rock. I was an emotional wreck.

I cried on the day of her death; I cried at the viewing, and I mourned at the funeral. The funeral brought me into the reality that she was really gone, but it did not bring closure. As I gazed at her lifeless body in the casket, I felt like the bond we shared was demolished. She loved me when my other grandmother hated me. She defended me when others accused me.; she thought about me and appreciated me when others demanded more of me. I cried while I made a tribute to her beautiful life. I was hurt, devastated, because it seemed the best part of me was gone. I remembered feeling scared like a child, longing for the warmth of her arms that always made me feel safe. And, that day, when I touched her, she was cold and gone. I wished it were fake, like a dream or daze. I thought, how could someone still exist and survive the pain I felt… it just could not be real.

That day, the longer I read her tribute, the more it became real. It almost felt like I was accepting her death in my words, although I did not yet embrace it in my heart. In the end, I was able to say to her, "thank you for accepting me and not trying to change me. Thank you for caring for me and for teaching me the life skills you did."

Three months later…

The death of my grandmother had sunk in, and we were spending more time with grandaddy. However, it was early days for us, as we were still learning to remember her without hurting all over again. We were simply being strong for each other. Then, just as we were barely progressing, illness struck.

Back in 2012, when my father lost his father, my mother's father was diagnosed with stage three lung cancer. He had coughed up blood, and we took him to the doctor. After several tests, it was confirmed that he had cancer. He went through chemotherapy for a year and continued to work. He always said, *"If I am not working, I am dead,"* thus he kept working. Granddaddy helped to care for granny up until her death. Even when she died, he was still vibrant and active despite his lung cancer progressing to stage four.

At age 77, the greatest man I knew lost his wife and still wanted to add value to the lives of others. Even in his seventies, he drove school buses and did community projects to help inspire others. He taught me how to iron, cook, handle a weapon, etc. After losing his wife, it was hard to keep granddaddy happy and cheerful. He started to go through similar patterns of depression as my other grandfather did when he lost his wife.

My grandaddy's health deteriorated exponentially fast due to the spread of the cancer to several other organs. I remember spending his last few days with him at the hospital. There he held my hand and told me the words I needed to hear. I still hear his voice reciting them to me, and they still move me every time I allow myself to listen to them. (Read his words in Chapter ### 'Cushions and Glimpses').

The deaths of my granny and grandaddy were huge losses to my family. Today we remember them in the legacies we have accepted and preserved in our own families. She was the one who introduced me to luxury cars and much of the finer possessions in life. But above all, she taught me how to love myself, my family, and my country. Grandaddy was a helpful, caring, philanthropic army veteran who believed in family and community. Today, I am no different. His teachings have added value to my life, community, and business.

***

By 2014 I had lost all my grandparents, and my life had changed dramatically. I had a daughter, and I was a single father. At that point, the three years' worth of loss had settled in, and I realized that I was now responsible for leading and caring for the family (meaning, my parents and sisters). The losses brought my family closer, even my parents. Although my mother had re-marry my parents also grew closer as friends. It almost seemed they should not have divorced. I respected my mother's husband, but it was also obvious, that my father's mother was the primary cause of them not being together. My sisters and I, and our parents were always close; however, I developed an even stronger bond with my father after the loss of my four grandparents. As a family, we spent more time together, especially me and dad. We watched sports together, and sometimes we did nothing, we just chilled together. Now, I do the same with my family. There is never too little time to connect with each other, and we are never too busy to drop what we are doing to get away together.

My dad died on May 31ˢᵗ, 2016, and nothing in the past prepared me for it. Then mom right after.

Mom had started living with Alicia (my sister who followed me) in 2014 due to her declining health. That same year (2014), so many other things were happening. I was praying for my mother and that God would bless me with a wife. I knew my daughter needed a female example in her daily life, so that was my priority. She had needs that only a mother could give, and I wanted her to lack nothing. (I believe that a mother and father are both vital to the development of every child, and no one person can perform both roles in their lives). I also wanted a wife from the motherland (Africa), so I asked God to bless me with a wife from Africa who would love my daughter unconditionally.

In the midst of that, my father was diagnosed with prostate cancer (in 2014). When I was in my early twenties, my father was more than a parent; he was my friend. During those years, I forced myself to give no regard to any possibility of losing him. When he passed away (from prostate cancer), my world shattered into a million pieces.

I thought I would be okay because he would be in a better place. But I was wrong. What I did not realize at the time was that my dad was not just my friend; he was my best friend. Dad loved the Word of God and often used it to address the issues of life. Although he was not always admired for his decisions, that did not dampen his influence in our family.

***

U p to 2015, my mother was progressing well until her health took a turn for the worst. She developed many complications, which were primarily due to her smoking over the years. That caused her to battle several other health issues. Nonetheless, she managed through debilitating pain, through every doctor's appointment until her very last day.

In the midst of what seemed to be waves of never-ending storms and short-term victories, God sent a ray of hope in the form of a woman named Gloria, who is now my wife. The Bible says, *"He who finds a wife finds a good thing, And obtains favor from the Lord."* (Proverbs 18:22). I, for one, can say a praying wife makes all the difference in a man's life. Our initial courtship was rocky. At best, Gloria had expressed no desire to give me the time of day because she had just finalized her divorce from her husband of 7 years. Yet, God gave me favor with her and allowed me to win her heart through laughter.

For the first time, I had someone who consistently and intentionally prayed for my strength. I was approaching the deepest pain I had ever felt up to that time, and God prepared help for me. Gloria prayed me through the pain of my father's death and spoke life into me. Now that I look back, I understand that everything was working cohesively for my good and purpose.

My mother's health continued to decline and, Alicia took excellent care of her. We talked every day, so it was normal for her to update me when there was any change, no matter how small. But on June 16, 2018, my sister called to say mom was not breathing.

"What do you mean she is not breathing," I asked.

She was like, "she is not breathing."

My sister had been doing CPR up to when she called to say mom had stopped breathing. Then when the paramedics arrived, they did an electrical charge to try to recharge her heart. They got a pulse, and we were elated, but I somehow knew that I needed to prepare myself for the worst. But I couldn't. I refused to regard the possibility of losing her. It was easier for me to comfort my sister than face the reality that we may lose our mother.

My mother was taken to Cedar Sinai Hospital in Los Angeles, California. For two weeks, she was in and out of a coma, and any improvement in her condition kept fluctuating. So instead of the immediate shock of death, this time we were taken on a tug of war of worry, then hope, then fear, and back again. Going to and from the hospital was emotionally draining. It was a dark and devastating time for me. Not being able to change her health status and not knowing what to expect each time I went to the hospital. We wanted better results for mom, so we moved her to a hospital in San Diego, California, that her good friend Mary had suggested. Mom was improving, but her health had deteriorated badly while at the other hospital. After six weeks, mom transitioned on August 4th, 2018.

Our mother was the definition of devotion to family, just like my granny. However, when she died, my sisters were not ready to process her loss. I did not show much emotion because I was more grateful that they were no longer in pain. I knew I would miss her and that healing from the loss would be an internal battle. I knew that of all the deaths we had overcome, our mother's death would be the deepest wound. It did not take us long to accept it because we knew she was in a better place. Her death meant that it was time for us to redefine the legacy for the generations ahead.

It is often said time heals all wounds. Although I went through a whirlwind of pain and loss in what seemed like a never-ending calamity, I gently came to terms with the loss I had experienced. After a season of allowing myself to grieve, I realized that life must go on. It is incredible how the experience of loss can cause us to rise to a better version of ourselves. Even when I wanted to lapse into the pain of the past, the resilience of my mind spoke to my innermost being and dictated my actions. I became conscious that even though my father had passed, I should be grateful that he was present and even more grateful for my time with him. In those moments, we have the assurance that although the storm of life may rage, there is always the hope of newness in life.

The support of my wife strengthened my sister and me to go through another season of grief. Even though we were sad, we clung to each other during one of the most painful periods of our lives, and over time, we recovered through the support of Gloria, friends, and family. Their continued patience and love helped lead me to a place of confidence and belief that everything would be alright.

***

G loria, over the many storms, proved to be my ride-or-die in every situation. We had developed a *'Bonnie and Clyde'* relationship. After a few months of dating, I found myself falling head over heels in love with this African chocolate beauty from the motherland, sent to me by God. I had never been in a relationship where a person showed me unconditionally love and consistent support in every situation. I knew in my heart that she was the one. So, I made up my mind at that point that I couldn't let her slip through my hands like a grain of sand and be left with a hole in my heart that no one else had filled.

I was by no means husband material; neither did I possess the know-how or track record of a long-lasting relationship or be a husband. Not to mention she was previously the wife of a reverend. I honestly believe that my smile, physique, and swagger would have made her swoon and melt into my arms once I said those magical words, *"will you marry me."* To my dismay and shock, upon me asking, I was met with a resounding NO. She explained that it would be to our detriment for us to enter into marriage, knowing that I was not ready to take that step at that point and time in my life. I had lacked the mindset and financial capability to be the head of a household, let alone raise the two children from previous relationships. Although I was upset and became emotionally aloof, during my quiet time of solitude, I had to be honest with myself and accept that she was right.

In those moments of introspection, I was able to practically analyze the issues I was facing. At that time, I was moonlighting, working the regular nine to five. I worked Monday through Friday at minimum wage. At nights I utilized my skills as a sports coach and refereed on certain weekdays. I knew that by no means was my income enough to provide for the family I wanted. I remembered my granny's famous words, *"a man has to set the standard of his own worth and value or someone else will,"* and I knew I did not want that to happen to me. Gloria was making significantly more than me working as a nurse and had already acquired a doctorate in theology, although she was only 30 years old. On the other hand, due to a series of unfortunate events, I constantly had to put my goals and dreams on the back burner to assist my family and provide for my daughter. That made me realize I had to raise my standard to meet my family's high level of stability. It was at that moment I decided I wanted to earn a six or seven-figure income. I understood that meant that I would have to transition from an employee to an employer. Working in the regular nine-to-five would no longer cut it for me. I constantly felt drained and unfulfilled and barely had enough time or energy for Gloria or the two kids. Then I realized that I also didn't want to be the type of father or future husband that provided financially but missed out on the most important times of my family's lives.

Over the next few months, I dedicated my time to formulate a plan to make my dreams of financial freedom a reality. I delved into every book about entrepreneurship and financial freedom that I could get my hands on, and today the rest is history.

2015 was filled with the promise of new things to come. Things were finally looking up. Gloria and I finally got engaged after a few months. I was able to strategize a workable and sustainable business plan that I quickly set into motion. I had decided to utilize my skills in personal credit to form my business, which I named Mega Credit Boost Inc.

I registered my company and completed all the legal formalities to make it official. Then, I focused on advertising, used several methods to create awareness around my services. Gloria and the children also passed out flyers to promote the business.

Very soon, we had our first customer, and then the business began to boom. In the beginning, Gloria and I were able to handle the workload. I would put profiles together, and she would mail them out. However, as the business grew, so did the workload. In a short time, I had to hire help to complete the credit repair services we provided.

The growth of Mega Credit Boost created income and extra cash for us to venture into other investment opportunities. But what happened next would prove to be the darkest time in my life yet. I had gone through six consecutive years of devastating loss, but nothing compared to the distress I felt when my fiancé, our children, and I were homeless. I had decided to venture into an entrepreneurial partnership with someone I trusted. In fact, we had previously conducted business on several occasions together, and this time was no different. As expected, the project was a success; however, he disappeared when it was time for me to receive my share of the profits. From there, everything went downhill. I was angry and in shock at the same time because I had used extra funds and money for our bills to invest. I knew that the financial dividends would far exceed the initial investments; additionally, the return would have come in early enough to cover my bills without a hiccup in my household's financial stability. This cataclysmic turn of events left us behind on bills with no backup. Eventually, we were behind on rent, and very soon, we were without a roof over our heads. As a husband and father, I felt ashamed, hurt, and disappointed. We became homeless for about four months, and although my wife was working, it wasn't enough to make a down payment on a new place.

We were forced to live in a hotel. It was not the best, but the important thing is that we were together. Those days, some of the scriptures my father shared with me while he was alive became words of hope and fuel to continue. Sometimes, I felt out of control, as if something else was playing the game of life for me. Little did the circumstance know that trials and difficulties schooled me, so eventually, I would rise to win. I had lost so much before; this time, I was motivated to overcome.

Over time, I worked hard to repair our credit. As we gradually recovered, we were able to rent a house for our family and slowly get back on our feet. Our friends never left us. They were there when we lost our family, and they showed up when my family lost everything. They gave us money and certain things that we needed to get from one day to the next.

When we finally could rent a place, it was a humbling feeling – a quiet yet momentous occasion for Gloria and I. I remember Goria praying when we went to look at the house; she cried out to God and pleaded our distress to him. She told him we had gone through enough, and He must intervene. We truly had exhausted all. During our homelessness, she also suffered a miscarriage. It was devastating for her, but as usual, she pushed beyond the hurt to support the kids and I. The emotional pain had a constant presence; sometimes, we forgot that hurt was not the norm. But on that day, she stood in that house and prayed to God for the change.

The efforts God enabled us to make paid off. Our credit was good, and Gloria's mother lent us some money. Shortly after, we went into a rent agreement for the same house. We moved from being homeless to living in a hotel, then renting a house in a good part of Fontana, California, next to the golf course! Only God could have made it possible!

If you can change
your MIND,
YOU can change
anything.

- JULIUS HAMMOND

Today, I no longer approach business the way I did then. My circle is extremely small, and as usual, I exercise diligence and caution in all my business decisions. However, while I am always ready to go all-in, ultimately, my confidence is entirely placed in God's leading.

In retrospect, I understand that our experiences were perfectly designed to retrofit us with the learning we need. I also understand that our experiences are often rolled out in our lives as programs designed to advance us at a level higher than the previous. Now, I not only understand, I know that the layers of loss I experienced was my university training for my future.

In the next chapter, I highlight the highs and people who gave me glimpses of hope to cushion the lows in my journey.

CHAPTER 3

———————⊖———————

Cushions and Glimpses

"When thou passest through the waters, I will be with thee; and through the rivers, they shall not overflow thee: when thou walkest through the fire, thou shalt not be burned; neither shall the flame kindle upon thee." – Isaiah 42:2

W ho we are is packaged in the purpose that God gives to each of us, and it is through our experiences we gather the wisdom relevant to executing our purposes. As we go through these experiences, the journey is often less than pleasurable, and the tunnels are sometimes winding, looking like there is no end. But, as God carefully assigns our experiences, he gives us cushions of comfort to ease our weary feet, glimpses of hope that tell us he is watching, and people of purpose to guide us on the way.

I am grateful for the memories I still have of my early years as a child, before life's experiences changed my perception of people and my self-worth. I remember looking forward to and enjoying weekends with my other granny. The Lord inspired my granny to establish the love of family with which I now identify. Thus, the love infused in me helped me not to receive the negative behavioral patterns my father's mother showed me, even though it was consistently given.

My granny and grandaddy were (two of a few) people who contributed to my purpose in my life. I believe they were placed in my life to guide, protect and support me until the Lord was ready for me to take the reins to lead my own family. Like my father, they attended all my sporting events and never passed on an opportunity to take me somewhere with them. They kept their eyes on me, and when I became a teenager, they made it their duty to counsel me about girls and teach me house duties, manners, and common courtesies. Although I was not interested to learn at the time, their words stayed with me.

"Formal-education is important, and life-education is equally important. Formal-education will get you in the door, but life-education will keep you in the game." — Gloria Nunn

The self-worth and family values I have today are because of my granny. She taught me business skills and showed me how to leverage them to thrive and not just survive in life. My granny was the first to explain the importance of good credit to me and taught me how to repair and maintain it. She respected a formal education, but she always reminded us that *"Formal-education is important, and life-education is equally important."*

Words are powerful; they can make, break, kill and give birth. Over the years, I have heard it all. I was told I am smart by some and stupid by some. I was treated specially by some, while others treated me like I didn't belong. To most, I was caring and hardworking; to others, I was irrelevant. Nevertheless, I pushed past the pain by continuously steering toward a purpose-driven life.

After my grandmother, grandfather, and granny died, my grandaddy became my silver lining in the midst of the storm. Beside my grandaddy's hospital bed, I stood wondering if all he taught me would remain even after he had gone. I wondered how I would accomplish great things without him. He and granny were my rock, and I did not know how to play the game of life without them. Then, as if he were in my mind, my grandaddy took my hand, while on his death bed, and said:

*"Son, don't let anyone determine your life, or tell you who you are; only God can do that. You will continue to be successful, for no one can stop you but you. Remember, **the choice to succeed or fail is always yours**. Don't ever compromise your integrity for a dollar bill because you can always get that dollar bill back. Once somebody feels that you have no integrity, it's very hard to change their minds. If you lose twenty dollars today, you can make it back tomorrow, but if you lose your soul and integrity, it is near impossible to regain."*

I reflected on those very words at his funeral and decided it was time to step into my true identity.

***

The seed of faith and the belief in the Word of God was planted and watered in my life by my father. Although he did not stand up for his family the way I thought he should have, he was the one who gave me the most powerful words in life. The Word of God was an anchor to my father and a shield I think he sometimes hid behind. When we cohabited with his parents, he was the symbol of present help in times of trouble. When my grandmother made degrading remarks and treated me with disdain, he always had a fitting word from the scriptures to encourage me and soothe my pain. He could have chosen to say what was in his heart, instead, he always chose to give me the Word of God. There is an unexplainable power in the Word of God that cultivates a spirit of hope beyond every circumstance. My father sowed the seed of the Word of God in my life; today, the Word of God has defined the beliefs that have led to my actions.

***

There is a saying, "Good friends are better than pocket money," and my best friends Sim Alawode and Donovan Avant are the epitome of friends rare and true. We became friends when I was a teenager, and since then, we have remained close friends.

I remember while living with my father and his parents, the tension became progressively unbearable. Sometimes I had to leave for a few days. On one occasion, I could not do something my grandmother asked me to do, which resulted in me being mercilessly thrown out of her house.

She asked me to take her to the store just as I walked out the door to go to a job interview. I told her that I couldn't because I was already running late. In her mind, my response was disrespectful. As soon as I returned, she threw my clothes into the streets and told me I could not stay in her house. While I gathered my clothes, I remember thinking that I could only go to my friend's house. To this day, I am grateful that I had somewhere to go and someone who listened.

My friends not only know all my past, but they also experienced every part of it with me. They shared their homes, their food, and their family with me. They grieved with me as I lost grandparent after grandparent, mother and father, even when I became homeless with a daughter, son, and a fiancé. They understood that I was hurt when others called it teenage rebellion. When I left home (without telling anyone) as a young adult, they empathized, while others called it male ego.

I was never alone; my friends made sure of that. In times of crisis, they constantly checked on me and did what they could to make my burden lighter. Sometimes they insisted that I go out just to take my mind off the issues my family faced. They knew I was strong, but the consecutive losses weakened me beyond my expectations. In those trying times, I also embraced what I had because being alone would have made it more difficult to navigate.

The most profound memory I have of their impact on my life is how they got me to embrace and accept my hurt. They helped me to release my hurt without me even knowing that they were changing my life. My friends knew me well. They knew that I was very headstrong and that I never showed my emotions. They also knew that keeping in my feelings would simply be me turning a baby monster into a giant. So, they smartly engaged me in discussions about my emotions as the trials came one by one. They helped me face my hurt and helped me change an identical part of me by identifying with my pain and helping me to overcome it.

This book is also a symbol of my release. Me letting go of my past hurt and converting the trials into triumph and my test into testimonies for others to overcome. Today we are all responsible adult men, leading different careers, but the common fabric of loyal support and genuine love remains strong among us.

***

A s Gloria, our children, and I pushed through the despair of homelessness, I also had to bury my parents. As I shared before, I felt like I was not in control, as if the world which revolved around me was making a mockery of my life. We had lost our business investment; our credit was demolished, and it seemed we had nothing but death and debt. My wife, my children, my friends were all there. Gloria's mother supported us financially and helped us get back on our feet. Others such as Chuck and Barb Belk were also there; they spiritually watered and fed our souls. I remember receiving a card from Chuck and wondering if he had printed the words in the card specially for me because there was no way he could have found a card that spoke directly to my heart. That was another cushion of comfort and a glimpse of hope beyond the storms. This couple ministered to every aspect of our lives. They constantly prayed over me and encouraged and strengthened my wife through their love. There was a time when they showed up with five hundred dollars and said it was not much, but they hoped it helped. Perhaps they did not realize it, but they gave me a seed after I lost all I had planted. Other couples helped us financially, including Mike and Deb, Lorraine, and several others. Like the four friends who lowered their sick friend through the roof to see to Jesus, so was my family lifted by these genuinely caring human-angels.

Every time memory takes me back to what these people did in our lives; it reminds me that everyone has something that someone else needs. The unselfish willingness of the persons of purpose in my life helped my family to get up, stand up and walk out of our trials and tribulations, out of debt and distress.

***

F ollowing my mother's death, life played us harder as if we were now experts at its game. I had already lost my grandparents and both my parents, but the most challenging days were still ahead. I knew I wasn't a loser, but it seemed I was losing the game. Nevertheless, I still had hope because I was still in the game. By this time, it was 2019, my wife and I began having martial issues, which escalated quickly after I cheated. Again, God placed persons in my life to protect the purpose he had placed on my life, marriage, and family. Mr. and Mrs. Kelvin and Laquetta Simmons made my wife and me see the error in our ways. The process was not as easy as writing a sentence. It took many prayer sessions to get me to accept that I had done something wrong. To my knowledge, none of the men in my life as a child had done that. That meant I was enabling or creating a legacy and identity that was not aligned with who God made me to be. I was so embarrassed, but forgiveness and healing begin with being honest with oneself. The scripture implores us not to be ashamed; instead, we should be truthful and repentant. Kelvin and Laquetta helped Gloria and me confront the demons that came against our union and the ones we individually brought into the relationship. They used God's Word to help me understand my identity in God and my responsibility as a husband to my wife. I learned to embrace my role as the head of the household that my wife came first, then my children, then everything else. I remember realizing that a man who did not love his wife as Christ loved the church was cursed. I was failing at my efforts, no matter how much due diligence and business learning I applied. Life changed when I decided to love my wife with my life (loving my wife as God loves the church).

I take this opportunity to thank Pastor Kelvin and Laquetta Simmons. I bless their marriage ministry called *'The K.I.S.S.'* May God continue to use them to preserve marriages and families through the Emmanuel Fellowship Praise Church, in Ontario – a haven.

Before I formed a relationship with the couples I mentioned, my sisters also were my outlet. We were brought up to be there for each other, so this was no different. After the many layers of trials, there was also a point that I felt that I needed to be weak and vulnerable without feeling the need to be strong for anyone. Those couples were purposed to be in our lives. They gave me a safe space to let go of all that I had gone through. Their actions reminded me that I was not alone.

Alone is a place and a state the enemy likes to take those he attacks. He makes suggestions to us, skewing out thoughts and emotions with an alone syndrome. The enemy of our souls (Satan) makes suggestions to us, hoping we would visualize them and put them into action. The enemy wants to isolate and penetrate our minds, spirit, and possessions so he can sink us into his trap. But God is always ahead, and he always has a plan of success for us. God is still the lead game maker, and he deals us cards of love, unity, collaboration to help us win the ultimate game - life.

***

Sometimes we mistake the glimpses of hope as threats to our progress, not realizing they enable our wins. In the same way that the children of Israel saw the giants as a threat when they were servants securing their possession and purpose, we sometimes view our blessings as curses.

57

After the break up with my daughter's mother in 2007, I moved to live in Las Vegas with my daughter. The move felt like a fresh start and put me much closer to my mother's parents, who were living in Las Vegas at the time.

Although I needed the change in environment, my primary reason for moving there was to become a correctional officer. As soon as we moved, I began working on achieving my dream. I applied, passed the physical test, and got through to work in the jails. However, before I could start employment, they had to complete background checks on me.

One day, as I waited to hear when I should start working, I received a call from the investigator who said something had gone wrong. Before he could explain what happened, I told him that I knew I had no felonies or anything questionable in my past. He quickly assured me that my record was found to be clean and that I had nothing to worry about. I was relieved until he said that I still could not get the job because the company was on a hiring freeze and that the freeze would last at least three to four months. He also added that after the freeze, I could reapply. The issue with that was that the application process took approximately ten months. That meant I would have to wait a year before I had a chance.

I was very disappointed, but it was a blessing in disguise. If I had gotten my dream job, I would not have taken the step into entrepreneurship. I would not be the business owner, investor, and coach I am today. My life would not be the success it is today. What seemed like a loss was indeed a gift!

So many persons are still on a journey they should have already gone through and come out of. But they have not yet identified, come into contact, embraced, or opened themselves to their people of purpose so that they can be delivered. Deliverance takes the collaborative effort of people speaking the same language, pursuing the same goal, using the right tools.

All my people of purpose were revealed at the right time, but I had to exercise the will to receive what they had for me. Their help was like cushions of comfort that gave me those glimpses of hope in many seasons of darkness and despair. It must have been God who orchestrated such a watch over my life.

As a matter of fact, I did not realize how much they had helped until I went through and came out. Without a doubt, they were God sent, certain and sure. Their coming was not an accident; instead, it was the intentional move of God.

Every person who proved to be purposeful in my life, every cushion that comforted me, and every glimpse of hope was a reminder that I was still being purged in the refiner's fire. The fire was not reduced or the duration lessened, but God kept his eyes on me and gave me constant reassurances toward my victory.

CHAPTER 4

⊚

My Wife

This chapter is dedicated to my wife, my spiritual partner, best friend, and biggest cheerleader.

My beautiful wife Gloria Hammond the African Goddess!

When my wife came into my life, I did not know the tremendous blessing she would have been. I did not even realize it at that time, but now I can say without a doubt, God had planned her into my life for a purpose.

He prepared her for me and set me up for a greater end than my beginning.

Gloria and I met through an online dating platform. By then, I was a single-parent father, doing my best to care for and protect my daughter. She came into my life at the right time, which was just before my mother died. And although I didn't realize it at first, it did not take me very long to see that she was not just someone I wanted to be with but someone I'd rather have by my side in difficult times.

As the older generation in my family was leaving me one by one, the Lord knew my parents would not have been far behind. So, he brought my wife into my life to be my best friend, Godly guide, support, and the love of my life. I assure you; I would not have been able to handle the death of my parents the way I did, had it not been for my Gloria.

I have had many dark days, and Gloria was there, even before I made her my bride. Together, we have weathered the storm of homelessness, survived credit delinquencies, been strong through miscarriages, and overcame many setbacks. Through it all, my wife had my back, even when I did not deserve it. She complimented me even when I was not great and was always genuine and fair in her feedback.

Even when a poor business decision forced us to be homeless for a while, Gloria was by my side. When things got a little better, we had to live in a hotel, far less than desired. Regardless of the realities, she made me feel like I had provided Buckingham Palace, gardens, and all.

The qualities I admire the most about my wife are her honesty, love for God and people, and her strength. When everything seemed to be going wrong, she was the little glimpse of light that intimidated the darkness, no matter how much darker the circumstances got. One day, the negatives were so surmounting that they almost overwhelmed the positives. Gloria was there to remind me that she appreciated what I was doing and that many others would benefit from my work one day. At that moment, I felt like I was on my face suffocating in the pressures of life, and my wife resuscitated me.

Do you have one person in your life whose instincts are always on point? For me, my wife is that person. On several occasions, had it not been for my wife (prophetically) ministering to me, I would have made the wrong decision. Like my father, she loves the Word of God. She always has a smile and a scripture to address any issue and brighten any dull day.

Gloria shares an unselfishly intimate relationship with God. So even before we were married, she challenged me to make God more centered in my life and our family. Gloria never hesitates to share and engage me in Godly discussions. She continues to remind me of the power of the Word of God and how I am at liberty to them. Her love for and obedience to God sparked in me a burning desire to have a closer relationship with God. Spiritually, she is way ahead of the curve, yet very modest in the way she communicates her knowledge to others.

Of all she has done, one thing that drew me to her quickly was her unconditional love for my daughter. I had experienced the hate my grandmother had for my mother. So, as a single father, I prayed for a woman who would love my daughter as her own. She always found creative ways to communicate her love, teach a lesson, reprimand, and give praise.

There is never a dull moment with my wife. This Nigerian beauty is beauty, brains, and spirituality. She embodies a completeness that can only exist in the acknowledgment of one's imperfection. Yet, she seeks to be a better person every day. Gloria's whit and genuine reception will knock your socks off and make you feel right at home. The same unforced whit even in teaching is evident in her soon-to-be-published storybooks. That is only one of the ways my wife adds value to other people's lives. Persons she has read for are amazed at how effortlessly she crafts important lessons into interesting stories for both adults and children.

Regardless of our abilities individually and together, the foundation of our marriage is our belief that it is God's will for us to be together. Therefore, while we have our individual purposes, we also know that there is a purpose that together we must accomplish through our marriage. No wonder marriages are attacked all the time; we have had our fair share.

We almost lost our marriage to my infidelity. But, again, Gloria was to my rescue, turning to the one who had brought us together. There were times when my focus was elsewhere, but Gloria continued to be a spiritual cornerstone in our family. She helped me embrace my duty as the priest of our family and establish my spiritual independence to trust God completely.

God is my all. Full stop. And my wife is so much a part of me; she can't get any closer. If I were to choose another character for myself, I would instead choose to be her than anybody else in the world!

I love you, Gloria.

CHAPTER 5

R & R'

This chapter is about relationship with God and relationship in marriage. Regardless of the differences between a relationship with God and another human being, the principles for a successful relationship across the board are the same. Over the years, I have learned and understood that the foundation of marriage is God and that my relationship with God will set the tone in my marriage. Irrespective of our character, principles, or moral compasses, a God-centered relationship will always be more successful than a relationship without God at its center. In the same way our past influences our future, our relationships with parents, family, and friends, also influence the relationships we share with our spouses, be it in marriage or not.

I intentionally chose to put this chapter right after the chapter dedicated to my wife so you would better understand why we have the marriage we do. However, our marriage did not magically morph into a beautiful specimen of God's love. The only reason why we have the marriage we do is because God is in the midst, and we continue to work toward the love of God manifesting in us toward each other. Note, I said, "we continue to work toward..." That is because we are imperfect, and we are not always the same persons every moment. God is the only constant; he never changes. However, it took time, effort, patience, learning, and application to establish our decision to join as one.

It is said that *"the proof is in the pudding."* And indeed, it is, because only after the newness rubs off in a relationship with God or someone else, that can we experience what is under the surface and in the depth of both parties. Coincidentally or not, the words religion and relationship have the same three beginning letters. But certainly, what comes after will define different directions and experiences.

***

G rowing up, my father taught me the Word of God, but I did understand God's role in my life or know Him for myself. In other words, I did not have an intimate relationship with God. I did not know His voice, so I did not always know if His voice was the one in my head or not. I did not know His walk or presence, so I couldn't tell that He was always close by. The change in my relationship status with God is evident in all aspects of my life. It is the only constant that keeps me grounded and secured. It secures me as a husband, a father, and a businessman. My relationship with God empowers me to have vision and see it come to fruition, speak, and witness it coming to the past. An intimate relationship with God is the vehicle that drives my purpose in every way.

It is said that children live what they learn, not what they are taught. However, for me, this saying is true only in part. What I learned about marriage from my parents was perhaps not what they intended for me to learn, neither what I would have chosen for myself. Nevertheless, I learned what they lived, more than what they said, and it was evident in my previous relationships.

I believe that my parents' relationship was part of the reason why the relationship with my daughter's mother was so strained. Thankfully, that is not the life I am now living. The change took place after I met Gloria because she not only learned something different, but she also decided that she was going to live some of what she was taught. It took our own marriage almost failing for me to change the narrative for my children. I did not want them to see marriage the way I saw it displayed by my parents. Regardless of what my parents preferred, I learned what they showed me.

My marriage to Gloria could have ended in divorce like my parents' marriage. Had it not been for God and my willingness to change the narrative of my past, I would not be able to do differently for my children. I realized that if I wanted my children to have a better marriage, I had to teach them exactly what I wanted them to learn. That meant the way I lived would be their teacher.

As I grew closer to God, I understood that everything in us and around us has a beginning or foundation. As a plant germinates from a seed, all that exists naturally has a spiritual foundation and explanation. Therefore, whether we want to call the source of our life experiences mindset or karma, all is from a source not of the natural. Therefore, nothing happens or exists without first coming through a spiritual force. The amazing thing about this knowledge is that it empowers you to define that force, giving you the opportunity to determine your outcomes.

Gloria helped me set my gaze on God and established a consistent relationship of intimacy with Him. That led me to see God as the foundation and lead in my life, but it began with getting close to Him so that I could know Him in a personal way. Since God is also embodied in His Word, it meant that knowing the Word God would teach me more of Him. The more I read the Word of God, the more I learned how to use His Word to control my outcomes. It was like a domino effect; do that and this happens, do this, and that happens, and so on.

Jesus, the only perfect man, asserted that He only used the Words of God, His father. Therefore, how much more important is it for us as imperfect beings to do the same. The change in my relationship with God transformed my life and improved my marriage exponentially. The more I learned about God, the more I understood His Word and applied it to my life, and the better it became.

Being spiritually wealthy and healthy through an intimate relationship with God will also enable abundant wealth and health in the natural. I remember having been unfaithful to my wife and how it hurt us dearly. At first, I did not realize how it negatively impacted me until after I encountered God through His Word. During the time I cheated on my wife, I was very unsuccessful. That may not be the case for other men who have cheated, but certainly, they would be more successful than they were or still are. In fact, it is important for any husband reading this book to understand that they are blessed when they love their wives as God loves the church. To do less than the same is a curse. In retrospect, I realized I was depreciating rather than increasing in value. Only spiritual wealth through intimacy with God can cause a husband to learn to love his wife as God loves the church and give His life to save hers.

Additionally, being wealthy in the Spirit gave me the ability to define and dictate outcomes in my life. I became more proactive rather than reactive. Through the Word of God, I learn to pray more purposefully and speak His Word into situations to determine the outcome best for my family and me. Like me, my journey with God has helped define and establish a solid inheritance for many generations to come.

Indeed, it is only through a strong connection with God that I can and have dominion over the outcomes in my marriage, my family, and myself. As I continue on the path of becoming a firm spiritual cornerstone for my family, my wife remains my primary support and like-minded friend.

Every new day represents a day already defined and ready to be executed. The moment you awake today, today is already a reality. You can no longer plan for the current moment you are living, but you still have the opportunity to change every moment until you can change days, years, and generations ahead. Whether by your past, your own words, actions, or mindset you have defined today, know that you can still change the outcome after today. My change began with me, and my family's change began with me first. The change in my marriage began with Gloria and me. That means I have an important role to perform in the direction my life takes.

Once again, I acknowledge that you and I have the ability to dictate every day through our relationship with God. Yes, many have been successful without acknowledging God. Nevertheless, they have applied His principles. Why would you not want abundant success when God is above all? Why would you not want to secure more than success on earth? Having a relationship with God and applying His word means that you have lasting abundance, heritage, and a secured future with Him as well.

But change did not happen overnight. It took much before the change could be seen with the naked eye. After my marriage hit rock bottom, I still could not see where I went wrong. Like Saul on the Damascus Road, God met with me where I was through the voice of others. I readily accepted that there was a need for change, but it took much longer for me to accept that I needed to change. To my own detriment, I did not even realize that if I did not change, I would have forfeited my victory, even after so many invaluable life experiences. God, through my wife, inspired friends and pastors with a direct anointing to help marriages consistently serve the Word of God to me as the bread of life. As soon as I began to embrace the Word of God and allowed it to saturate my heart, my process of transformation and renewal began.

Improve your relationship with God; it will improve your life more than you imagined.

- JULIUS HAMMOND

CHAPTER 6

───────⊘───────

Exhausting All

A gain, Miles Monroe once said,

"The wealthiest place in the world is not the gold mines of South America or the oil fields of Iraq or Iran. They are not the diamond mines of South Africa or the banks of the world. The wealthiest place on the planet is just down the road. It is the cemetery. There lie buried companies that were never started, inventions that were never made, bestselling books that were never written, and masterpieces that were never painted. In the cemetery is buried the greatest treasure of untapped potential."

When taking a road trip, the first thing you do before leaving is fill your tank with enough gas for the journey.

And if you run low or empty on the way, you make it your responsibility to refuel before proceeding. Likewise, you have been blessed with resources within and outside of you to fuel your journey. Should you refuse to use your fuel, you will never keep moving forward or even backward. For, believe it or not, we need fuel to go back as much as we need it to go forward. So, since you can't have your cake and eat it, you also cannot get to your destination and still have the **same** full tank of fuel. In fact, if you still have the same full tank and you end up in another place, it would mean that the world shifted and you are dead.

Unlike the dead, you are one hundred percent alive and have the opportunity to empty yourself by reserving nothing to fulfill your purpose in life. As a matter of fact, if the analogy of the full tank and fuel is too much to handle, consider this. If life is truly a game, tell yourself you are *going all-in* - intentionally giving all, leaving no room for *'nothing.'* In that case, exhausting your all means you have taken all avenues, giving of yourself completely and uncompromisingly to achieve an identified outcome. And while to everyone else, you may be bluffing, to you, your next move is an ace toward your win. Therefore, never ever see your efforts as a gamble or a bluffed play. See your life as a performance that you are *'faith-ing'* all the way.

 the primary mastermind and
 killer of talent, potential, and
 pletely vulnerable to receive the
 equires you to show up without
 rrassed to learn.

Myles Munroe, Les Brown, and many others have emptied
their gift of motivational speaking, pouring the wisdom
they have been given into others and allowing themselves
to be filled by others on their journey to emptying. These
men have motivated many persons to empty while they
themselves were doing the same. As it is said, so many
businesses never started, so many goals never
accomplished because those who are dead allowed fear to
be greater than their faith. We were not made to simply go
through the motion of life and be led wherever it takes us.
No. We're meant to define life for ourselves, exceed in joy,
excel in wisdom, and receive the abundant life God gave
us.

The principle of giving and receiving is not just a
phenomenon of man's experience; it is a divine principle
taught in the bible. Yet, so often, persons say they have
nothing to give, which is not true. And, others, like the man
who hid his one talent, say they have only one thing, so
they can't afford to give it away. However, many persons
do not realize that masters focus on one target in

establishing their greatness. Hence, in giving, you need only one to generate a return.

To exhaust all, you must use all the resources you have been given. Like the car on a journey, the fuel you have is to propel you forward. Like the car, when you are empty, you will be filled. Sometimes we do not want to give our all. Often in fear of not having fuel for the rest of the way. However, it is in giving our all that we will be filled. The Word of God assures us that we will receive a return when we give; therefore, we should not hesitate to give the same complete effort to our goals and decisions even if the last attempt was a lesson instead of a win. Sufficing to say, so many persons miss out on the win because they stopped at the learning. It is your learning that will move you forward or promote you to another level.

Not everything we hold on to is needed. And everything we don't need is useful to someone else. As humankind, we gather so much, yet we hardly pour out to relieve ourselves of the baggage. Begin to make room for new opportunities by giving your time, your resources your knowledge. The more you offload, the more you make room for your new needs to be filled. Remember, as humans, we change and grow. If we do not empty, there will be no room for us to feed or aid our growth.

Whether you are serving physically, investing money, giving yourself to others, or being vulnerable in a conversation, you reserve nothing for yourself when you give your all. Exhausting your all involves your mind, body, and spirit, making one hundred percent effort toward the same goal. So, regardless of the capacities, you are required to exist in, your willingness to exhaust all will determine how full your life is lived. Therefore, the more you empty, the more you will be filled.

CHAPTER 7

―――――⊖―――――

Layers of Learning

Time always tells!

Time allows us to reflect, introspect, and identify the lessons and apply the learning from our experiences. It brings us to a place where we don't just have the knowledge but also acquire the understanding that in every experience, there is certain learning to take us closer toward our win!

I would never discount the efforts of those persons who chose a professional path. Equally, I must respect those who identified that their family personally needed them more than a career. However, the learning I want to share with you is the learning taught in the classroom of life.

I was not always this positive, not even close. In fact, for a long time, I wondered why I had to go through so much to achieve a goal… only time could tell, and time did tell. It took years for me to understand the mysteries wrapped up in my experiences. And even longer for me to process how grateful I should be.

Now I know that learning is a process and a journey toward wisdom. And while we all have the ability to learn, learning becomes much harder when we face challenging or adversarial circumstances. Hence, to learn, we must first create an environment of learning, where our mind and body understand that we will not give regard to fear or feeling. Instead, we will view every aspect of the challenge we face as a part of our success package.

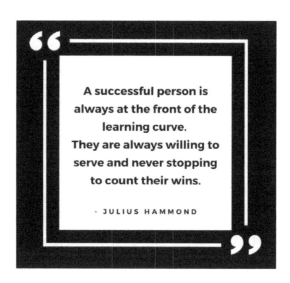

A successful person is always at the front of the learning curve.
They are always willing to serve and never stopping to count their wins.

- JULIUS HAMMOND

Acknowledging that my past was designed for my success led me to discover that any change in my life must start with me. It caused me to take on a *'Me First'* approach. 'Me First' felt like the game-changer. I knew that to effect the change my life and purpose required, I had to wipe the slate clean and be willing to start over. Starting over was not new for me because I did not just lose my grandparents and parents. I had lost the columns to my heritage. I started over when I lost my four grandparents in the space of 4 to 5 years. And before I could settle down with my parents, they passed, and I was handed the mantle, still at a young age. Therefore, it was clear that I had to be first in many respects. First and foremost, I had to be willing to be the first to fail (which genuinely is not a failure but learning), me first being positive, me first owning a business, me first being married, me first to reconcile, me first in my family to write a book, among other firsts, too many to mention.

Not everything I was first in was pleasant or desirable, but being first also puts me first in line for the wisdom to teach others. As I challenged myself at showing up first, I became less shy and more open to emptying all of me every day. It caused me to approach every challenge with an attitude of gratitude and a willingness to learn more than win. I was so focused on learning; I hardly paused to celebrate the wins because I knew once I was learning, that the wins would automatically follow. Ultimately, my focus, discipline, and actions became more purposeful.

Do you know why your change will always begin with you? It begins with you because:

YOUR change will
start when YOU
CHANGE your
MIND.

- JULIUS HAMMOND

Was there ever a time you wondered when it would be your time to shine? Continue in your processing; because the challenges you face today represent success progressing toward you. Someone once said, *"The best victories come in the most unattractive packages. And, when they show up, we miss them because they do not look the way we expect."*

I call my past my gift, most of which I have shared in this book. If you change your perspective and begin to view your challenges as gifts, you will see their packages. Sometimes the packages are people we trusted who let us down, or circumstances taking unexpected turns for the worst. Do not respond via your sense of feeling. Remember, as a human, your automatic response is to get discouraged. But you can change that narrative and apply one hundred percent of you. Anything less will devalue your effort, yielding you depreciating results. Do not consider your efforts a gamble. By genuinely embracing your gifts, you will realize they are diamonds set in the ruff for you.

The next lesson I learned was that change was a personal journey and not necessarily for me and my family or relatives. My family was my core support system. They were all I knew and all I had. They defined my values and helped shape my decisions. From my granny to my father, every part of me could be found in one or another. It took me becoming a single parent, losing my parents, meeting the woman of my dreams, and almost losing her to awaken my identity hidden down on the inside of me. The layers of loss slackened my hold on everything and made me realize the importance of making every moment a joyful experience. But first, I needed to identify my identity to establish my [own] house, my [own] family.

Having a grandmother who was relatively negative in her interaction with me, a mother who did not realize its impact on me, and a father who did not verbally defend me made me realize that only I could control how things impacted me. I also realized I had to decide what I would regard enough to allow inside me and what I would not regard enough to be recognized. Yes, I recognized everything, but I only regarded some and recorded only the important parts. Those parts that were positive, the parts that confirmed what the bible said about me, those parts that confirmed the person I dreamt of becoming.

The experience with my grandmother caused me to learn how important it was for me to be motivated from within. In the beginning, I went through a roller-coaster of anticipation and disappointment. On a regular basis I had to do many things for her, especially when my parents divorced and she lived with my father and I. During those years, I hoped doing good to her would make her treat me better next time, but I was always disappointed. Sometimes when she sent me to the store or asked for her meals, I thought she would have a change of heart when she saw how much value I added. I always got a rude awakening. The constant disappointment wearied me until it defined in me the ability to focus only on the things that mattered.

Over the years, my father had a major impact on me, and only time could unveil this understanding. I was upset at his neglect, but a more important lesson was existing in the midst. My father did not verbally defend me, but he always noticed my hurt and used the scriptures to encourage me. I did not realize it at the time, but my father was sowing seeds inside of me. The scriptures were stored in my internal hard drive and later became the fuel behind unveiling my identity and realizing personal victory. My father's counsel helped me to love my grandmother, although I understood that she hurt me. Over time, I also had to conclude that although my father gave me an invaluable gift, I could not be loyal to his legacy. He did not defend his family, and I was determined to do otherwise (without disrespecting him).

Growing up as a child, I thought the separation between my parents was very unfortunate and unfair. Today, As Gloria and I continue to grow in my own marriage, I am still learning many of the lessons taught years ago. One unmentioned reason why my parents separated is that they did not understand their roles and responsibilities to each other as defined by God. Even though my father often quoted many scriptures, he lacked understanding and application of the same. However, I deem it a privilege to have witnessed his errors to avoid the same today. In fact, I have a responsibility to do better, having been given the opportunity to do better – *("But he that knew not, and did commit things worthy of stripes, shall be beaten with few stripes. For unto whomsoever much is given, of him shall be much required: and to whom men have committed much, of him they will ask the more. - Luke 12:48)* I also have the responsibility to teach my children through my action and words. For this reason, I am further motivated to develop a relationship with God's character through His Word. It is important that the character of God defines and shapes our character as husband, wife, son, daughter, sibling, countryman, and humankind.

To catalyze my change, I had to learn how to forgive as often as I had the memory of the hurt. And beyond forgiveness, I had to learn how to define ALL aspects of my past as a blessing. Notice I did not mention the opposite. That is because it has no place in describing my past. Therefore, when you are humiliated, experiencing loss, hurt, or pain, remember to apply the keys to your deliverance: love, forgiveness, gratitude, respect, and fervent prayer.

The key to not regarding any iniquity in your heart is to believe that all that comes in contact with you came through God's divine permission. Remember that God assures us through His Word that His thoughts toward us are good and not evil *("For I know the plans I have for you," declares the Lord, "plans to prosper you and not to harm you, plans to give you hope and a future." -* Jeremiah 29:11- NIV). Regard every challenge as your benefit by loving those who hurt you and respecting them as a vessel God uses to bless you. Accept your challenges as lessons to advance you in to your purpose. And firmly believe that something great is nestled in every experience regardless of how negative.

I believe that through every challenge, God is training you to be tested for a higher level. So, sit every test in sight of your promotion. Knowing that even if it turns out to be a mess and not a test, there's a message that God is trying to give to you in the midst of your mess.

I encourage you to hold firm your experiences, the pleasant and the not so pleasant ones. And after you have endured, remain in place to receive the delivery and remain still enough to hear the message. When you have received it, cherish and relish it, protect and preserve it. For in your struggle, no lack or loss, struggle or triumph could shift your resolve to learn, overcome and be victorious!

Finally!

No, not quite yet. There is one aspect I deliberately did not share. It is about going back to acquire respect and regard before you are launched into the fullness of your abundant purpose.

In Luke 2: 40-52, we see the story of Jesus going back. In verse 40, we first see him as a strong child, full of wisdom, teaching doctors and perhaps professors. A few verses later, he had to go down/back to be subjected to his parents. In the end, Jesus increased in wisdom and stature and favor with God and man.

(Julius going back story) After meeting Gloria, I had to go back to where it all began. I was in Las Vegas, and I wanted to stay there, but I had to be pulled back once more for the grand launch into my future.

Going back is designed to increase you in wisdom and character and give you dominion in the eyes of all people in your past, present, and future. So, when you go back, remain focused because it is in going back that your regard and respect will be established.

Whether you go back to your hometown or the place where you experienced much hurt, remember, going back will be different. You will not understand why you are back, but if you apply the learning, you have just acquired, your before and after will not be comparable.

CHAPTER 8

Who I am

The evolution of my identity began on March 30th, 1984, when I was only Julius Hammond, son of Wendy Rachelle Nunn and Joe Lee Hammond Jr. Today, Julius Hammond is only my name, but 'Who I am' is the identity that possessed and now lives inside and outside of me. My identity is blueprinted in my capacity as husband to Gloria Hammond, as a father, friend, and businessman. These are a composition of the blueprint God gave me. The ability to exist in these capacities [the way I do] is defined by my relationship with God and who He has made me to be.

I never understood 'who I am' until after I recommitted myself to my marriage. In fact, six years into our marriage, my wife confronted me about my relationship with God and how much I was leaving on the table not being close to Him. As usual, she explained the importance of a relationship with God and committed herself to helping me get there.

Ten years ago, I was a different Julius. Then, I was defined by the streets; every other word out of my mouth filthy without purpose. Until one day, I asked myself if this was all I was going to be. My parents were still alive, but I was bitter, broken, and still grieving the loss of my granny, who meant the most in life to me. By the time I lost my father, I had met my wife, but still not sure who I was supposed to be by her side. Over time, I immersed myself into the Word of God and listened to persons whose lives were transformed by the renewing of the mind and not being afraid to give one hundred percent effort, even in areas where they seemed to have failed.

A lot of my reshaping came through shifting my perspectives regarding my past and letting go to make room for new drive and fuel to propel me forward. In being reshaped, I had to be willing to put all into having an open mind so I could embrace new understanding. I had to be willing to forgive completely and embrace the learning that came with every experience. In the very beginning, I wondered why I was going through the pain of facing the hurt of the past and bothering to forgive over and over again. As I trusted the transformation process, I realized that in time I would see the bigger picture. I started to embrace every obstacle as an opportunity for progress and every learning as a valuable part of my win.

Besides the fact that I am a husband to Gloria (a part of my identity), a father, brother, friend, credit coach, and investor, who I am will continue to be defined by God's eternal presence in my life!

Epilogue

Full Life

Our expectations are sometimes shattered simply because we keep forgetting that all cards (good, bad, and indifferent) are dealt from the same deck. Similarly, our experiences are not always what we prefer, but if we look closely, they are designed to teach us wisdom relevant for our future.

I was not always a confident experience-loving person. However, there is an unexplained peace when you come into a relationship with God. It is that peace that is described in Philippians 4:7.

"...the peace of God, which passeth all understanding, shall keep your hearts and minds through Christ Jesus." – Philippians 4:7.

I consider my life an experience filled with opportunities that I prefer to call layers of learning rather than layers of trials. The successful imperfect work-in-progress that I am is because of the wisdom teaching experiences with which God has

blessed me. The gift of life is from God, and he is the ultimate dealer. He blesses us with experiences that will teach us and cause us to grow. He will never teach or test us in an area of strength, simply because he intends for us to grow rather than simply be sustained.

> *"We grow only from our weaknesses. Our strengths can only sustain us"* – Giannah Smith

Whether we see life as a game or a journey, it is important to note that we are the ones playing the game. The cards are simply the vehicle to our wins, and we can't win without them. Similarly, we can't learn without experiences, so why not embrace them and gain the benefits?

When Jesus was twelve years old, he already knew his purpose – 'he was here to do the will of the father.' Although he was God, and he knew how to navigate the realm of the spirit, he still needed to learn how to fulfill his purpose as a human/flesh. Jesus needed to acquire the learning so he could execute his ministry in the future. The story is detailed briefly in Luke Chapter 2. Jesus' parents were on their way home when they realized that he was not with them. While his parent searched for him, He was teaching academic scholars and men renowned in their careers. When His earthly parents found him, they questioned why he was not with them. His response was not one any child who knew better would give. Already this tells us that Jesus, who was God, made flesh, was indeed a child and needed more experience before he could start his ministry.

Although Jesus was technically competent to teach lawyers and doctors (who obviously would have been older than him), he needed to learn and be touched with the feelings of children and not only adults. Between the book of Luke and John, we realize Jesus spent the rest of His childhood and some of his adult years subjected to His parents. He needed a child's experience, a teenager's experience, and an adult's experience so that he could minister grace at every level. Later in his life, we would see him delivering the young as well as the adult. Luke chapter two ended by saying that,

> "And Jesus increased in wisdom and stature, and in favor with God and man." Luke 2:52.

Sometimes the cards life deals us are hard to play. Sometimes it seems like our experiences are all the same. It can even feel like life is unfair. This book is about my wisdom teaching experiences packaged as layers of trials. Trials that today define who I am and the impact that I make. I have learned to be strong and courageous, giving my all without regret. For to hold back is to rob myself of the learning nestled in every experience.

Every poker game is different, as is every experience, but always remember that the cards dealt come from the same deck, that even with a bad hand, we can always try a bluff and see where life takes us.

> *"The strengths of successful people are sustained by their choice to intentionally challenge their weaknesses."* – Giannah Smith

Sometimes you only show your cards after the win. So, do not be afraid to play your bluffs; they are your faith plays, much of which you will need every day. Give life your all, hold nothing back in fear, for you may regret not experiencing the fullness of your purpose on this earth. For it's when you have done your share when you have exhausted all; God steps in to do the rest. Remember, your best is always possible. So, after you have done your best, your faith in God will do the impossible.

I have learned much from my struggles and from the people who supported and continue to support me that there is a surmounting of blessing for every single hurdle. And what I find about blessings is that they don't all come in a rush every time. They simply come at the right time.

Relieving yourself of your past through the renewal of your mind is not an easy task. It takes a fervent and intentional resolve to unmask yourself to reveal your true identity. It requires a consistent intimacy with God, in whom your true identity resides.

The answers are in you. Let go, retrain your mind, and remember that you can only die empty if you continue to give yourself completely, for you are the most important part of your change.

I am delighted I had the opportunity to share my experiences with you. I hope my testimonies will support your overcoming and lead you to emptying yourself daily so you can be filled. I pray my sharing blessed you beyond possibilities, beyond your vision, and even beyond your eyes can see.

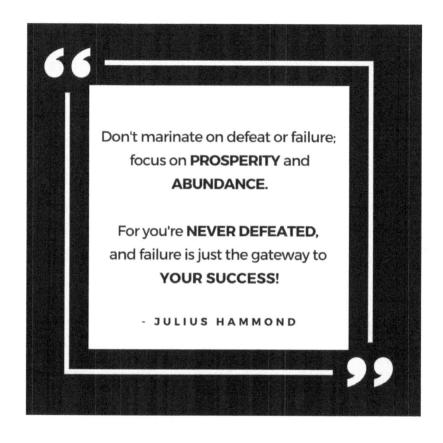

Don't marinate on defeat or failure; focus on **PROSPERITY** and **ABUNDANCE.**

For you're **NEVER DEFEATED,** and failure is just the gateway to **YOUR SUCCESS!**

- JULIUS HAMMOND

A Note To Myself

Hey Jrock,

The journey has been long, and you've won many rounds. The road may have been rough, but you have triumphed and have kept your feet on the ground.

Keep the faith, and continue to grow from your weaknesses. For you will succeed at any and everything you put your heart, mind and soul into.

Peace.

Acknowledgement

I first and foremost, give thanks to my Almighty, Savior Elohim, Yeshua, Jesus Christ for life, every learning, and every win. I am deeply grateful for the opportunity to serve you through my story and help you overcome through my testimony.

My deepest gratitude goes to my wife, confidant, and best friend, Gloria Hammond. Her inspiration and support were pivotal in my change from just living to have an abundant life in all respects.

I thank my daughter and son, Samarah Hammond and Israel Oketola. I am truly grateful to my sisters, Alicia Hammond and Brittney Mashell – Nunn who love and support me unconditionally.

Heartfelt and boundless gratitude to my friends, Simeon Alawode, Donovan Avant, and Chuck and Barb Belk. They have not just been there during the rough times, by they have held me up even when they also need a hand.

The princess, Samarah Hammond.

The prince, my son Israel Oketola.

A big thank you to my support team, who collaborate to ensure my family I are always covered. To Chuck & Barbara Belk (Ministry Leaders and Good friends).

*My Sister Alicia Marie
Hammond*

*My sister Brittney-
Mashell Nunn*

Gloria and I thank La Quetta Bush Simmons & Kelvin Simmons (Pastors & Counselors), who were instrumental in restoring our marriage. They counseled us and made us realize that life is worth living together. The demonstrated and helped develop in us the oneness that should exist in marriage, as the church is in Christ.

I thank everyone who has been inspirational, prayerful, and resourceful in the growth and development of who I am today. Thank you, and God Bless you

***

I also pause to acknowledge the deceased but not forgotten souls from my family.

Wendy Mashell - Nunn

Joe Hammond Jr.

Gloria & Zellars Nunn

Delores & Joe Hammond

About Author

Julius Hammond's life is a success story woven by layers of loss, love, and gratitude. He has encountered many highs and lows, ebbs and flows, all characterized by learning toward his win. In his memoir, a work of deep reflection and shared learning, Julius invites readers into his world, chronicling the experiences that have led him to identify where he came from and who he is —from his childhood to his years of loss, marriage, entrepreneurship, homelessness, and success. Wisdom teaching and revelatory, Julius' story is a profoundly personal reckoning of depth in life's untold lessons.

Today, Julius Hammond's success is represented in the maturity of his struggles and a crafted mindset worthy of raising the standard of life for generations beyond. In under 10 years, Julius Hammond has mastered success in business from the position of gratitude, perseverance, discipline, and action. As CEO of Mega Credit Boost Incorporated, Hammond teaches people how to live and lead a better life. Known for his passion for serving others,

Hammond constantly seeks opportunities to demonstrate the value in exhausting all in every effort and learning from every experience.

Contact the Author:

YouTube: Julius 'Kingjrock" Hammond

Instagram: megaboostinc

FaceBook: Mega Credit Boost, Inc

Website: www.megacreditboost.com/

JULIUS HAMMOND

Your Notes

Your Notes

Your Notes

Your Notes

Your Notes

Your Notes

Your Notes

Made in the USA
Las Vegas, NV
06 December 2021

36277958R00075